THE LITTLE RED BOOK OF
COWBOY WISDOM

Edited by

STEPHEN BRENNAN

Introduction by

Johnny D. Boggs

Skyhorse Publishing

Skyhorse Publishing books may be purchased in bulk at special discounts for sales promotion, corporate gifts, fund-raising, or educational purposes. Special editions can also be created to specifications. For details, contact the Special Sales Department, Skyhorse Publishing, 307 West 36th Street, 11th Floor, New York, NY 10018 or info@skyhorsepublishing.com.

Skyhorse® and Skyhorse Publishing® are registered trademarks of Skyhorse Publishing, Inc.®, a Delaware corporation.

www.skyhorsepublishing.com

10 9 8 7 6 5 4 3 2 1

Library of Congress Cataloging-in-Publication Data is available on file.

ISBN: 978-1-62636-079-2

Printed in China

CONTENTS

INTRODUCTION

By Johnny D. Boggs

In May of 1999, I worked on a cattle drive, moving about a hundred head of Herefords and a few longhorns to their summer pasture in Arizona's White Mountains. That's not something I do every day, but I had a magazine assignment, and, as a Western novelist, I wasn't about to pass up on that experience.

About halfway through the drive, as I mounted my giant horse, Jack, my camera slid over my shoulder and slammed into Jack's neck. The rodeo began. No time for that, cowboy. I went sailing, but—not wanting to be left afoot—I snagged the reins, holding on as I slammed into the ground.

It wasn't my first horse wreck. Nor would it be my last.

Quickly, I got up, calmed down Jack, and checked my camera, which was fine. The only thing injured was my pride, plus that leather burn across my palm since I hadn't put on my gloves. Looking around, I realized I had been blessed. Nobody had noticed, too busy looking after the herd or their own horses. I climbed back in the saddle and resumed my position.

The following evening, as we gathered around a campfire, honesty got the better of me. Some of the cowboys were joking about another rider who had been spilled. "That's the only rodeo we've had on this drive," a grizzled cowhand said while drinking coffee.

"No," I admitted sheepishly. "Jack bucked me off the other day."

Everyone stared at me. Then, the veteran asked, "Did anyone see it?"

"No, sir," I replied.

"Well." He sipped his coffee. "If nobody saw it, it didn't happen."

Such logic appealed to me. That's the kind of wisdom only a veteran cowboy could acquire.

Over the years, I've interviewed, befriended, studied, written about, and ridden with many cowboys and ranchers. One pulled his partial from his mouth to show me his latest badge of honor. Another, recovering from a bad wreck, waxed philosophical: "Never been hurt, never been horseback." Which was the first thing that came to my mind in the Ruidoso, New Mexico, emergency room when the doctor told me after my latest up-close-and-personal look at cowboying, "Two fractured ribs. You're in for a fun six months. Stay off horses for a while."

In this *Little Red Book*, Stephen Brennan has captured the cowboy's wisdom, and you don't have to be a cowboy to relate to many of these pearls.

Brennan draws from movies like *Will Penny*, one of Hollywood's most accurate depictions of the cowboy and perhaps Charlton Heston's best performance. Kirk Douglas has said that his favorite role was as Jack Burns in *Lonely Are the Brave*, based on Edward Abbey's novel *The Brave Cowboy*. Joel McCrea often considered his occupation to be rancher, not actor.

Brennan relies on cowboys who earned their fame in other fields. Eugene Manlove Rhodes cowboyed for twenty-five years in southern New Mexico and drew on that experience when he turned to writing. *Copper Streak Trail* and *Pasó por Aquí*—the latter turned into one of my favorite Western movies, *Four Faces*

West—helped Rhodes become known as "The Bard of the Tularosa." Charlie Russell left his Missouri home when he was sixteen, bound for Montana to become a cowboy. And he did, working in the Judith Basin while painting and sculpting on the side before turning to art full time. Today, Russell's paintings and bronzes continue to inspire artists, art lovers, and Western aficionados.

Some of the quotes are humorous. "Never follow good whiskey with water, lessen you're out of good whiskey," an unknown cowhand once observed.

Others are deadly serious. "Most men are more afraid of being thought cowards than of anything else, and a lot more afraid of being thought physical cowards than moral ones." That's from *The Ox-Bow Incident*, Walter Van Tilburg Clark's first novel, which put two drifting cowboys, Art Croft and Gil Carter, in the middle of a lynching. A classic indictment of mob law—I first read it in my junior year English class in high school—it was turned into a powerful Western film in 1943 starring Henry Fonda.

Yet funny or serious, anonymous or known, these sayings all show just how wise cowboys (real, wannabe, or pretend) could be. And still are.

I grew up in South Carolina during the tail end of the Western TV boom. *Gunsmoke* was a Monday evening routine. On our elementary school playground, we reenacted *The Gunfight at the O.K. Corral*, despising Martha Knight, who had traveled to Tombstone on summer vacation and had the audacity to inform us: "It didn't happen that way at all!" I played hooky my senior year in high school to watch *Fort Apache*. My bookcases and DVD cases overflow with Westerns. *Log of a Cowboy. These Thousand Hills. The*

Introduction

Time It Never Rained. The Rounders. Hell's Hinges. Red River. My Darling Clementine. Jubal.

Children today may not have that connection I had growing up, but whenever I walk into a grammar school or library in boots and cowboy hat, those boys and girls—and often the adults, too—get excited. The cowboy remains an iconic American figure.

Perhaps my biggest pet peeve is when I read or watch something about "The End of the West" or "The Last Cowboy."

The West isn't over, and cowboys are still working on ranches, herding cattle. When I walk into the local grocery, I'll often see a dusty cowboy in a battered hat and scuffed boots. The West remains a vibrant land, full of mystery, danger, beauty. The cowboy remains a key ingredient of this wonderful country.

And the cowboy's wisdom endures.

PART 1

WHOOPEE TI YI YO, GIT ALONG, LITTLE DOGIES

*(Traditional song intended as accompaniment
to the motion of the slow walking gait
of the saddle on the trail.)*

As I walked out one morning for pleasure,
I spied a cow-puncher all riding alone;
His hat was throwed back and his spurs was a-jingling,
As he approached me a-singing this song:
Whoopee ti yi yo, git along, little dogies,
It's your misfortune and none of my own,
Whoopee ti yi yo, git along, little dogies,
For you know that Wyoming will be your new home.
Early in spring-time we round up the dogies

Mark 'em and brand 'em and bob off their tails;
Round up our horses, load up the chuck wagon.
Then throw the dogies upon the trail.
It's whooping and yelling and driving the dogies
Oh how I wish you would go on along;
It's a whooping and punching and go on little dogies,
For you know that Wyoming will be your new home.
Some boys go up the trail for pleasure,
But that's where you get it most awfully wrong;
For you haven't any idea of the trouble they give us,
While we go driving then all along.
When night comes we hold them on the bed ground,
These little dogies that roll on so slow;
Roll up the herd and cut out the strays,
And roll on little dogies that never rolled before.
Your mama she was raised a -way down in Texas
Where the Jimson weed and the saddle burrs grow;
Now we'll fill you up on prickly pear and cholla
'Til you're ready to trail to old Idaho.
Oh, you'll be soup for Uncle Sam's Injuns;
"It beef, heap beef," I hear them cry,
Git along, git along, git along little dogies,
You're going to be beef steers by and by.

• • •

PART 2

TENDERFEET

"Horses?"
"Yeah, horses. You know. The things you fall off of."
—*RIDE, RANGER, RIDE*
(1936)

• • •

"I like a damned fool," he hissed, "but you suit me too well!"
—EUGENE MANLOVE RHODES
THE TROUBLE MAN

• • •

How to ride a horse: First, you mount the horse. Second, you stay mounted.
—Proverb

• • •

He couldn't hit the ground with his hat in three throws.
—Anonymous

• • •

Never slap a man who's chewing tobacco.
—Anonymous

• • •

If you do get thrown from a horse, you have to get up and get back on, unless you landed in cactus; then you have to roll around and scream in pain.

—Anonymous

• • •

Bill stared at him. "Does your mind hurt your head?" he asked
solicitously.
—Eugene Manlove Rhodes
The Trouble Man

• • •

Kings and cowboys I have known, and the cowboys stand above
the rest. I am six thousand miles from them at this moment
and fifty-six years in time, but they seem nearer to me than this
morning's newspaper.
—Frank Harris

• • •

Never approach a bull from the front, a horse from the rear, or a
fool from any direction.

—Proverb

• • •

Once I knowed a clodhopper that made his self a rawhide hat. It worked fine until one day he got caught out in the rain. Then the sun came out and that hat drawed up so tight he couldn't git it off. And it was drawin' up and mashin' his head somethin' terrible. Lucky for him it wasn't far to a tank, and he got off and stood on his head for a few minutes and it come right off.

—MODY C. BOATRIGHT
PECOS BILL TALES

• • •

There are three kinds of men: Those that learn by reading, and the few that learn by observation. All the others only learn by peeing on an electric fence.
—UNKNOWN

• • •

It's easiest to eat crow when it's still warm.
—UNKNOWN

• • •

It ain't enough for a man to learn how to ride; he must also learn how to fall.
—MEXICAN PROVERB

• • •

If you haven't made up your mind, don't use your spurs.
—Proverb

• • •

Mister, I wouldn't set that coal-oil on the stove. It ain't judicious.
—Anonymous

• • •

A smart ass doesn't fit in the saddle.
—Unknown

• • •

A man, a horse, and a dog never tire of each other's company.
—Proverb

• • •

Never miss a chance to shut up.
—PROVERB

• • •

Wipe off your chin.
—UNKNOWN

• • •

"Leo," said Jeff, "you're a good boy—a mighty good boy. But I don't believe you'd notice it if the sun didn't go down till after dark."
—EUGENE MANLOVE RHODES
THE TROUBLE MAN

• • •

Don't leave your saddle out in the rain.
—UNKNOWN

• • •

When you lose, don't lose the lesson.
—PROVERB

• • •

Don't squat with your spurs on.
—ANONYMOUS

• • •

Just 'cause a chicken has wings don't mean it can fly.
—PROVERB

• • •

Don't fret about biting off more than you can chew; your mouth's
likely a whole lot bigger than you think.
—UNKNOWN

• • •

Remember, silence is sometimes the best answer.
—PROVERB

• • •

PART 3

HORSEFLESH

We were riding west, making seven or eight miles an hour. I was
on my favorite buckskin horse. This horse was good in every way,
a fast runner, a fine saddle horse and faithful.
—H. H. HALSELL
GOOD SAMARITAN COWBOYS

• • •

A man who rides a good horse is usually a good man.
—ANONYMOUS

• • •

Cowboys call skill with horses "being handy."
—CHRIS IRWIN
HORSES DON'T LIE

• • •

There's no secret so close as between a horse and rider.
—PROVERB

• • •

I don't think it's nice you laughin'. You see, my mule don't like
people laughing. He gets the crazy idea you're laughin' at him.
No, if you apologize, like I know you're going to, I might con-
vince him that you really didn't mean it.
—JOE
A FISTFUL OF DOLLARS (1964)

• • •

You can tell a real cowboy by the way he sits his horse.
—PROVERB

• • •

"Range hosses," says Rawhide Rawlin, "don't ask nothin' of men.
Since Cortez brought them, they've been takin' care of themselves. . . . Wolves don't have much chance. Hosses stay in bands—
if a wolf or wolves show up, they won't run like other animals,
they bunch; and range hosses are dangerous at both ends, strikin'
and kickin'. A wolf likes somethin' easy. After he feels the hoof of a
range mare a few time, he quits—it takes his appetite away."
—CHARLES M. RUSSELL
RANGE HORSES

• • •

The mares would take a dislike to the stallions if we cut their tails.
They would lose their respect and affection for them, and would
not recognize them as their stallions.
—AN OLD VAQUERO

• • •

Cowboys . . . each have to undergo much hard toil . . . on account
of the extreme slowness with which everything must be done, as
trail cattle should never be hurried.
—THEODORE ROOSEVELT

• • •

It is recorded in Genesis' act of creation that man was given dom-
ination over all animal life. In circuses this record seems to be
verified. Sometimes, however, it pays to let a good horse have his
way, and sometimes it pays to follow a dog's trail. I have known
occasions when good common horse sense was sadly lacking in
irresponsible man. A good, faithful, well-trained horse will not
forsake his owner, and wherever the footsteps of man have trod
the dog has been his faithful companion.
—H. H. HALSELL
THE TRUE COWBOY

• • •

When your horse dies, get off.
—PROVERB

• • •

The word "bronco" comes from the Spanish word for "rough."
—UNKNOWN

• • •

Mounted on my favorite horse, my lariat near my hand, and my trusty guns in my belt, I felt I could defy the world.
—NAT "DEADWOOD DICK" LOVE

• • •

"The worst hoss I ever rode," said Bowlegs, "I rode because I had to. It was a case of ride or lose my locks, an' I'm still wearin' hair."
—CHARLES M. RUSSELL
A PAIR OF OUTLAWS

• • •

HORSEFLESH

(*Sheriff fires at the murderer,*
who attempts to escape on Gene's horse)
"Hold it, Sheriff!"
"But he's got your horse!"
"That's his hard luck."
(*Gene whistles and Champion wheels and*
returns the killer to the posse)
—THE GENE AUTRY SHOW
(1950)

• • •

As long as wild horses are galloping free,
I'll dream of the West as I want it to be.
—RITA AND CHARLES SUMMERS

• • •

I prefer a safe horse to a fast one—I would like to have an excessively gentle horse—a horse with no spirit whatever—a lame one if he had such a thing.
—MARK TWAIN

• • •

It's a little like nut and bolts. If the rider's nuts then the horse
bolts.
—NICHOLAS EVANS

• • •

An' I'm here to tell these machine-lovers that it will take a million
years for the gas wagon to catch up with the hoss in what he's
done for man. To-day some of these auto drivers want to kill him
off to make fertilizer out of his body. Mebbe I'm sentimental, but
I think it's a damned hard finish for one that has been as good a
friend to man as the hoss.
—CHARLES M. RUSSELL
RANGE HORSES

• • •

I got a horse for my cowboy . . . best trade I ever made!
—ANONYMOUS

• • •

Real cowboys don't never run away. They ride away.
—PROVERB

• • •

Certainly the opening of the western frontiers of America was made possible by horses that were ridden and packed under the saddle and those that worked in harness.
—ANDY RUSSELL
HORSES AND HORSEMEN

• • •

This outfit had an old mule which used to be worked on the mess wagon but now was on the retired list. But come what may, he'd still follow the outfit faithfully. From dawn till dark, from range to range, there he was, trailing close behind.
—BOB KENNON
SOME COOKS I HAVE KNOWN

• • •

Every fall from a horse makes you just that little bit wiser.
—UNKNOWN

• • •

In backwoods justice, horse stealing was worse than man-slaughter and a frequent occasion for lynching. To call a man a horse thief was the ultimate insult.
—DEBORAH EVE RUBIN
HORSE TRIVIA, A HIPPOFILE'S DELIGHT

• • •

Never was a horse that couldn't be rode. Never was a cowboy that couldn't be throwed.
—TRADITIONAL SAYING

• • •

When I was a kid, if a guy got killed in a Western movie, I always
wondered who got his horse.
—GEORGE CARLIN

• • •

He's what you call an educated bucker. He don't fool around with
no pauses. He jest starts in and figgers out a situation and then gets
busy slidin' the gent that's on him off'n the saddle. An' he always
used to win out. In fact he was known for it all around these parts.
He begun nice and easy, but he worked up like a fiddler playin' his
favorite piece, and the end was the rider lyin' on the ground.
—MAX BRAND
THE QUEST BEGINS

• • •

When you are young and you fall off a horse you may break
something. When you are my age and you fall off, you splatter.
—ROY ROGERS

• • •

In horse vernacular, Roy has always "given me my head," and I
have tried to do the same for him.

—DALE EVANS

• • •

There has been much said about pack-ponies, and that method
of working a range, by taking grub on a pack. Some very amusing
things will occur with the pack. I remember once, while driving
through Waco, the pack-pony became a little unruly, and was running up and down street after street, when the pack slipped and
turned under. This put the little gentleman to kicking. The result
was that flour, bacon, beans, tincups and plates, coffee-pot, sugar,
onions and bedding were strewn over about five acres of ground.
Some of the boys suggested that we hire the ground broke and
harrowed before it rained and thus secure a good crop of grub.

—W. S. JAMES
STYLE ON THE RANCH

• • •

You live in hell? I ride him every day!
—PROVERB

• • •

Hosses love pure cold water. In running water, which they like best,
most of them drink with their heads up stream, every hoss tryin'
to get above the rile. I've seen bands of hosses at a prairie spring
waitin' their turn to drink where the water was cold and clear.
—CHARLES M. RUSSELL
RANGE HORSES

• • •

"Good ride, Cowboy!"—What a good metaphor for life.
—BOB DOYLE

• • •

When you count your blessings, count your horse twice.
—PROVERB

• • •

There are few things more exciting than releasing a band of young horses from a corral where they have been confined for some time into open space and watching the explosion of movement as these meteors take an open country.
—THOMAS MCGUANE

• • •

If your horse don't want to go there, then neither should you.
—PROVERB

• • •

Yes, fellers, that's the worst hoss I ever forked, but that same roan packed me many a hundred miles to safety, an' as I said before, gentle hosses is all right, but give me a snakey one for a hard ride.
—CHARLES M. RUSSELL
A PAIR OF OUTLAWS

• • •

Don't spur a willing horse.
—PROVERB

• • •

A good horse is not very apt to jump over a bank, if left to guide himself; I let mine pick his own way.
—BUFFALO BILL CODY

• • •

HORSEFLESH

Ain't nothin' like ridin' a fine horse in new country.
—Augustus McCrae
Lonesome Dove by Larry McMurtry

• • •

The best thing for the inside of a man is the outside of a horse.
—Anonymous

• • •

The horse when roped by the head if wild, will choke himself down and the best method of holding him when once down is to take him by the ear with one hand, nose with the other. To illustrate, if the horse falls on his left side you want to take hold of his ear with your right hand and nose with your left, raising it until his mouth is at an angle of forty-five degrees, placing one knee on his neck near his head. In this way a small man can hold a large horse on the ground.
The difference in holding a horse and cow down is that you must hold the horse's front legs or head on the ground because he never gets up behind first but throws his front feet out and then gets up; the cow on the contrary gets up directly the reverse, gets up on her hind feet first, therefore you must hold her down by the tail. The horse is easily choked down but it is almost an impossibility to choke a cow down.
—W. S. James
Style on the Ranch

• • •

Life is short. Ride your best horse first.
—Proverb

• • •

There's something about riding on a prancing horse that makes
you feel like something, even when you ain't got a thing.
—Will Rogers

• • •

The horse you get off of is not the same as the horse you got on.
It is your job as a rider to ensure that as often as possible, the
change is for the better.
—Cormac McCarthy
Cities of the Plain

• • •

If you can lead it to water and force it to drink, it isn't a horse.
—Anonymous

• • •

I go about looking at horses and cattle. They eat grass, make love, work when they have to, bear their young. I'm sick with envy.
—SHERWOOD ANDERSON

• • •

Sometimes you ride hard, sometimes you ride easy.
—TRADITIONAL COWBOY SAYING

• • •

Whoever said a horse was dumb, was dumb.
—WILL ROGERS

• • •

"I like that horse more than anything in the world, but if he wants to go, he should be free."
"Him a beauty. Like mountain with snow—silver-white."
"Silver. That will be a name for him."
—JOHN REID AND TONTO
THE LONE RANGER
(1949)

• • •

He won't be coming back to his stable no more
My loyal horse, he won't be coming back, no!
He won't be neighing with joy anymore,
As he did when I caressed him.

Curse be the bad luck
That suddenly took him away, Oh!
My poor bay horse,
How I cried when he was no more.
—A VAQUERO'S LAMENT
"MI CABALLO BAYO"

• • •

If it can't be done from a horse, it probably ain't worth doing.
—UNKNOWN

• • •

When I hear someone talk about a horse or a cow being stupid, I
figure it's a sure sign that the animal's out-foxed them.
—TOM DORRANCE

• • •

Life's never so clear as when seen from the back of a horse.
—Proverb

• • •

No hour of life is wasted that is spent in the saddle.
—Winston Churchill

• • •

Ain't no way you can impress a horse—or a good friend.
—Proverb

• • •

So long! If I don't come back the mule's yours.
—Eugene Manlove Rhodes
The Trouble Man

• • •

PART 4

SIX-GUN COWBOY

The sun was near the meridian when Johnny rode into Gunsight,
a town which he took as a matter of course. They were all alike, he
reflected. If it were not for the names they scarcely could be told
apart—and it would have been just as well to have numbered them.
—CLARENCE E. MULFORD
BIT BY BIT

• • •

Sometimes you get, and sometimes you get got.
—ANONYMOUS

• • •

"You ain't never gonna get me alive to Fort Grant, boy."
"Then I'll get you there dead . . . boy."
—JED COOPER ANSWERS MILLER
HANG 'EM HIGH
(1968)

• • •

The revolver is a pistol with a rotating cylinder containing five or six chambers, each of which discharges through a single barrel. It is six pistols, encompassed in one, commonly know to its familiars as a "gun," "six-gun," "shooting iron," "six-shooter," or "Colt." The Colt was the original revolver, so far as American history is concerned, and it furnished the principal upon which all other models were constructed."
—WALTER PRESCOTT WEBB
THE STORY OF THE SIX-SHOOTER

• • •

He's yellow as mustard, but without the bite.
—ANONYMOUS

• • •

"When a man with a .45 meets a man with a rifle, the man with the pistol will be a dead man. That's an old Mexican proverb . . . and it's true."
—RAMON
A FISTFUL OF DOLLARS
(1964)

• • •

Best to drink your whiskey with your gun hand, to show your good intentions.
—UNKNOWN

• • •

Knowin' this feller's back history, I ain't takin' no chances. I see his right hand drop; the next thing I know he's on the floor with a bunch of screamin' women over him, an' I'm backin' for the door with a smokin' gun.
—CHARLES M. RUSSELL
A PAIR OF OUTLAWS

• • •

I would like to see every woman know how to handle firearms as naturally as they know how to handle babies.
—ANNIE OAKLEY

• • •

You may need me and this Winchester, Curly.
—RINGO KID
STAGECOACH
(1939)

• • •

As we go to press, Hell is in session in Ellsworth.
—KANSAS *STATE NEWS*, 1873

• • •

Every time you shoot at someone, plan on dying.
—NAT "DEADWOOD DICK" LOVE

• • •

I heard God's fast.
—BILLY
PAT GARRETT AND BILLY THE KID
(1973)

• • •

My mother and sisters thought my prowess with the gun was just
a little tomboyish.
—ANNIE OAKLEY

• • •

Never run a bluff with a six-gun.
—BAT MASTERSON

• • •

"I say Mr. Hickok, how many men have you killed to your certain knowledge?"
"I suppose I have killed considerably more than a hundred. And not one of them without good cause."
—Attributed to Wild Bill Hickok

• • •

You shoulda shot that fella a long time ago.
Now he's too rich to kill.
—Chill Wills

• • •

"What's that fellow wanted for, Sheriff?"
"Murder! If you see him, shoot first and shoot straight!"
—Tumbling Tumbleweeds
(1935)

• • •

Diplomacy is the art of saying
"Nice Doggie" until you can find a rock.
—WILL ROGERS

• • •

"You haff last request?"
"Sure would like me a chew of tobacco."
—*HANG 'EM HIGH*
(1968)

• • •

If I was you, I'd let them shoot it out.
—BUCK
STAGECOACH
(1939)

• • •

Where population is sparse, where the supports of conventions and of laws are withdrawn and men are thrown upon their own resources, courage becomes a fundamental and essential attribute in the individual.
—WALTER PRESCOTT WEBB
THE GREAT PLAINS (1931)

• • •

"I think you're walkin' into a trap."
"That's my responsibility, Autry."
"Sure, but we're with you."
—*RIDE, RANGER, RIDE* (1936)

• • •

"Somebody after you?"
"Three somebodies."
"The Law?"
"Naw, this is personal."
"I don't want 'em to catch up with you here."
"I don't want them to catch up with me anywhere."
—THE MARSHAL AND JIMMY RINGO
THE GUNFIGHTER
(1950)

• • •

I'm on my best horse, and I'm goin' at a run, I'm the quickest
shootin' cowboy that ever pulled a gun.
—TRADITIONAL
THE OLD CHISHOLM TRAIL

• • •

Aw go to hell, you long-legged son of a bitch.
—TOM O'FOLLIARD, AFTER BEING MORTALLY
WOUNDED BY SHERIFF PAT GARRETT, 1880

• • •

I early in my career recognized the fact that a cowboy must know
how to use his guns, and therefore I never lost an opportunity
to improve my shooting abilities, until I was able to hit anything
within range of my .45 or my Winchester. This ability has times
without number proved of incalculable value to me, when in
tight places. It has often saved the life of myself and companions
and so by constant practice I soon became known as the best shot
in the Arizona and pan handle country.
—NAT "DEADWOOD DICK" LOVE

• • •

"Say, that reminds me, weren't you in that dice game when
Norton was killed?'
"Now, Gene, you don't think one of us daylighted Ed?"
—*THE GENE AUTRY SHOW*

• • •

Our orders are to make sure he does not die . . . but also to make
sure he regrets the day he was born.
—CHICO
A FISTFUL OF DOLLARS
(1964)

• • •

In camp was found a book, the first of the kind I had ever seen, in
which I was made a great hero.
—Kɪᴛ Cᴀʀsᴏɴ

● ● ●

"You're going to shoot us ain't you, Chisum?"
"I thought about it. Then I thought about something Henry
Turnstall once said. He watched a man walk to the gallow . . . saw
him hang. He said it was ghastly. Well, I've seen men hang, and
that's the word—ghastly. You two are going to hang."
—Cʜɪsᴜᴍ
(1970)

● ● ●

Here I lay me down to sleep
To wait the coming 'morrow.
Perhaps success, perhaps defeat,
And everlasting sorrow.
But come what may I'll try it on,
My condition can't be worse,
If there's money in that box,
'Tis money in my purse.
—CHARLES "BLACK BART" BOLES,
NOTORIOUS STAGECOACH ROBBER

• • •

I am not afraid to die fighting, but I would not like to be killed
like a dog unarmed.
—BILLY THE KID, IN A LETTER, 1879

• • •

"How'd you know when he was gonna draw?"
"By watchin' his eyes. Remember that."
"I will."
—TOM DUNSON TO THE BOY MATT GARTH
RED RIVER
(1948)

• • •

"Well, don't you like my looks?"
"I don't see nothing the matter with your looks. Should there be?"
—CLARENCE E. MULFORD
BIT BY BIT

• • •

Brother, when I hit 'em, they stay hit.
—GABBY HAYES
BORDERTOWN GUN FIGHTERS
(1943)

• • •

Better not carry a six-shooter till you learn to shoot. You'll be a living temptation to some bad man.
—Attributed to Buffalo Bill Cody

• • •

"Now turn around and head for the door. Keep movin' and don't do anything sudden with your hands."
"I'll be seeing ya, Mister Ringo."
"All the way outside, sonny."
—Jimmy Ringo and Hunt Bromley
The Gunfighter
(1950)

• • •

I won't give up my guns, an' you won't lynch Hopalong Cassidy while I can pull a trigger. That's flat!
—Clarence E. Mulford
Hopalong Nurses a Grouch

• • •

Whenever he gets low in spirits or confused in his mind, he doesn't feel right until he's had a fight. It doesn't matter whether he wins or not. He feels fine afterwards.
—Art Croft
The Ox-Bow Incident
by Walter Van Tilburg Clark

• • •

You lose a lot of time reachin' up to it. Now lower your holster until the grips just touch the palms of your hand as they hang naturally. But your main fault is that you're watchin' my hand. Never mind this hand, just keep your eye on the spot you want your bullet to go to. Your eyes stay focused on this spot as your gunsight comes up. The instant that gunsight reaches the lower portion of the spot, you fire—but not before.
—Wyatt Earp to Bat Masterson
The Life and Legend of Wyatt Earp
(1956)

• • •

I regard myself as a woman who has seen much of life.
—BELLE STARR,
SHORTLY BEFORE HER MURDER IN 1889

• • •

If lawyers are dis-barred, and clergymen are de-frocked, don't it
follow that cowboys are de-ranged?
—UNKNOWN

• • •

What's the use of looking on the gloomy side of everything?
—ATTRIBUTED TO WILLIAM "BILLY THE KID" BONNY
AS TOWN-FOLK GATHERED TO SEE HIM HANGED

• • •

With a gun in his hand, nothing stands in his way.
—Don Miguel Rojo
A Fistful of Dollars (1964)

• • •

Aw, you ain't worth killing.
—Billy the Kid
to John Chisum, over a debt

• • •

"Riding long?"
"Since I started."
"Going fur?"
"'Til I stop."
"Where do you belong?"
"Under my sombrero!"
"Ain't mad are you?"
"Not yet."
—Clarence E. Mulford
Hopalong Nurses a Grouch

• • •

The Bible says when a man smites you on one cheek to turn the other, so I done that. Then I didn't have any further instructions, so I used my own judgment!
—EUGENE MANLOVE RHODES
AFORESAID BATES

• • •

"He don't look so tough to me."
"Well if he ain't so tough, there's been an awful lot of sudden natural deaths in this vicinity."
—*THE GUNFIGHTER*
(1950)

• • •

Dodge City is the one town where the average bad man of the West not only finds his equal, but finds himself badly handicapped.
—Andy Adams
The Log of a Cowboy (1903)

• • •

Are you gonna pull them pistols, or whistle Dixie?
—Clint Eastwood
The Outlaw Josey Wales
(1976)

• • •

Anger is a killing thing: it kills the man who angers, for each rage leaves him less than he had *been* before—it takes something from him.
—Louis L'Amour

• • •

My father, J. G. Hardin, was a preacher and circuit rider. He was a strong, God-fearing man who carried his Bible like a six-gun and fought with the Devil wherever he found him.
—JOHN WESLEY HARDIN
THE LAWLESS BREED
(1953)

• • •

No Ranger retires perpendicularly.
—NASH CRAWFORD
THE OVER THE HILL GANG
(1969)

• • •

When you are throwing your weight around, best be ready to have it thrown around by somebody else.
—UNKNOWN

• • •

God better have mercy on you. You won't get any from me.
—The Sheriff
The Ox-Bow Incident
(1943)

• • •

Perhaps I may yet die with my boots on.
—Wild Bill Hickok
(He did actually die with them on.)

• • •

You know how it works, Jake, you ride with an outlaw, you die with an outlaw. I'm sorry you crossed the line.
—AUGUSTUS MCCRAE
LONESOME DOVE BY LARRY MCMURTRY

• • •

How come I've got to run into a squirt like you nearly every place I go these days? What are you trying to do? Show off for your friends?
—JIMMY RINGO
THE GUNFIGHTER
(1950)

• • •

Don't shoot me! I don't want to fight!
—BILLY CLANTON
BEFORE OK CORRAL GUNFIGHT

• • •

Listen, your job is to back me up, because you'd starve without me. And you, your job is shut up.
—BUTCH CASSIDY
BUTCH CASSIDY AND THE SUNDANCE KID
(1969)

• • •

"I'll swear you in. Do you?"
"I do."
"You are."
(Hoss is reluctantly sworn in as temporary Deputy Sheriff)
—ERIC "HOSS" CARTWRIGHT
BONANZA
(1959)

• • •

I don't back down from any man, unless he was my pa.
—JOHN WESLEY HARDIN
THE LAWLESS BREED
(1953)

• • •

From the moment I slapped eyes on this hombre, I smelled trouble. And refried beans.
—*MAVERICK*
(1994)

• • •

You have to look pretty fast to see the bullet that gets you.
—GENE AUTRY

• • •

"You call that justice?"
"Justice is the handmaiden of the law."
"You said law was the handmaiden of justice!"
"Works both ways."
—PAUL NEWMAN AS ROY BEAN
THE LIFE AND TIMES OF JUDGE ROY BEAN
(1972)

• • •

My mama always told me: never put off till tomorrow people you
can kill today.
—Attributed to Doc Holliday

● ● ●

Speak your mind, but ride a fast horse.
—Proverb

● ● ●

Last night Bill Hickok, better known as "Wild Bill," acting sheriff of the county, while attempting to preserve peace among a party of intoxicated roughs, or "wolves," shot a man named Bill Melvin through the neck and lungs. Melvin is still living, but the doctors say, with no hopes of recovery. He attempted to shoot several citizens, and was determined to quarrel with everyone whom he met, using his revolver freely, but fortunately injuring no one.
—*HAYS CITY, AUGUST 24, 1869*

• • •

"Judge, you didn't give him no chance."
"He didn't deserve a chance. If he wanted a chance, he shoulda gone somewhere else."
—*THE LIFE AND TIMES OF JUDGE ROY BEAN*
(1972)

• • •

A gun is a tool, Marion, no better or no worse than any other tool, an ax, a shovel or anything. A gun is as good or as bad as the man using it. Remember that.
—*SHANE*
(1953)

• • •

When a man's got money in his pocket, he begins to appreciate peace.
—*A FISTFUL OF DOLLARS*
(1964)

• • •

I'm peaceful. My han's are up, palm out.
—CLARENCE E. MULFORD
BIT BY BIT

• • •

If you're hit and go down, you gotta kill him in the next instant or
you'll be killed. It's your life or his—aim right at his heart.
—WYATT EARP
THE LIFE AND LEGEND OF WYATT EARP

• • •

Cries for help are frequently inaudible.
—TOM ROBBINS
EVEN COWGIRLS GET THE BLUES

• • •

And in the end you wind up dyin' all alone on some dusty street.
For what? For a tin star. It's all for nothin.' Will, it's all for nothin.'
—HOWE
HIGH NOON
(1952)

• • •

Won't some of you good people get him up off the ground and into it.
—Pat Garrett
Pat Garrett and Billy the Kid
(1973)

● ● ●

"Your days have come to an end."
"My days?! What about yours, gunfighter?"
"The difference is I know it."
"So what do you propose we do about it? Hand over our guns to the bartender and start harvesting potatoes?"
"Not just yet."
—Shane and Riker
Shane
(1953)

● ● ●

I've never committed a cold-blooded murder in my life, and I'm not about to. Not until I find Maverick.
—*MAVERICK*
(1994)

• • •

Fast is fine, but accuracy is everything. Take your time. It's important to draw first and get off the first shot, but it's much more important to have your shot go where you want it to go.
—ATTRIBUTED TO WYATT EARP

• • •

Don't put on that badge until Halloween.
—ROY ROGERS TO SHERIFF CAROL
HELDORADO
(1946)

• • •

Git a rope.
—ANONYMOUS

• • •

PART 5

ON THE TRAIL

Let's ride, gentlemen.
—Captain Wilson
Hang 'Em High
(1967)

• • •

It was a hard land, and it bred hard men to hard ways.
—Louis L'Amour

• • •

The best way to get a hand to do something is to suggest he's too old to do it.
—UNKNOWN

• • •

Sage brush is a very fair fuel, but as a vegetable it is a distinguished failure.
—MARK TWAIN

• • •

I'm back in the saddle again.
—GENE AUTRY

• • •

If you don't meet the devil now and then, you're traveling in the
same direction.
—PROVERB

• • •

The horse wrangler had charge of the horse herd, or remuda. The
horse wrangler has no prestige.
—WALTER PRESCOTT WEBB
THE GREAT PLAINS

• • •

The old West is not a certain place in a certain time, it's a state of mind. It's whatever you want it to be.
—Tom Mix

• • •

I wanted to be a cattle rancher when I was young because it was what I knew and I loved it.
—Sandra Day O'Connor

• • •

If you're not making dust, you're eating it.
—Proverb

• • •

Cowboys at work, eighteen hours a day, for the herd left the bed ground by daybreak and kept until dark; cowboys at work, riding, singing, nursing the cattle; yet it is difficult for those who now read of their hardships to realize that they worked at all.
—WALTER PRESCOTT WEBB
THE GREAT PLAINS

• • •

Ese fue un supo.
That was a lucky throw.
—A MEXICAN VAQUERO

• • •

Just because it's a well-marked trail, doesn't mean whoever made
it knew where he was going.
—PROVERB

• • •

When my time comes, just skin me and put me up there on
Trigger, just as though nothing had ever changed.
—ROY ROGERS

• • •

They are universally acknowledged to be the best hands that can
be for the management of cattle, horses, and other livestock.
—A TEXAS SETTLER

• • •

Gonna see a man about a horse.
—UNKNOWN

• • •

"We're just passin' through."
"Well, next time you go around."
—JOSEPH "LITTLE JOE" CARTWRIGHT TO A SQUATTER
BONANZA
(1959)

• • •

We made more money feeding molasses, urea, and corn cobs to
cattle than we ever did feeding dent corn.
—ORVILLE REDENBACHER

• • •

No chaps, no slicker, and it's pourin' down rain,
And I swear, by god, I'll never herd again.

Coma ti yi youpy, youpy ya, youpy ya,
Coma ti yi youpy, youpy ya.

Last night I was on guard, and the leader broke the ranks,
I hit my horse down the shoulder and I spurred him in the flanks.

The wind commenced to blow, and the rain began to fall,
It looked, by gab, like we was going to lose them all.

I herded and I hollered and I done very well,
Till the boss said, "Boys, just let 'em go to hell."
—TRADITIONAL
THE OLD CHISHOLM TRAIL
COLLECTED BY JOHN LOMAX
(THE RHYTHM IS SAID TO MATCH A HORSE AT A JOG-TROT.)

● ● ●

'Bout as easy as milkin' a bull.
—Anonymous

• • •

A man, a horse, and a dog, never weary of the other's company.
—Proverb

• • •

Hi-ho, Silver, away!
—John Reid
The Lone Ranger
(Radio; 1949)

• • •

"Just gonna make some java. Care to join me?"
"Not me, your coffee'd throw a horseshoe."
—*The Gene Autry Show*

• • •

A bad day roping beats a good day at any other work.
—TRADITIONAL COWBOY SAYING

• • •

Western fieldwork conjures up images of struggle on horseback.
—STEPHEN JAY GOULD

• • •

"Spider venom. It keeps us safe from the wolves and wild dogs."
"Colt 45 will do the same thing."
—JOSEPH "LITTLE JOE" CARTWRIGHT ANSWERS TIRZA
BONANZA
(1960)

• • •

Lord, please help me, lend Thine ear,
The prayer of a troubled cowman to hear.
No doubt my prayer to you may seem strange.
But I want you to bless my cattle range.
—FROM *THE COWBOY'S PRAYER*

• • •

You look at a herd of cattle and well, they all look the same . . .
but they know. They all have an individual personality, and
those personalities change from day to day. They can have their
grumpy days and their happy days and their serene days. But it's
unpredictable. You can't be off in outer space when you're dealing
with animals.
—Chris Cooper

• • •

In ranch work, the cutting horse is used to sort out unproduc-
tive cows from the herd, to separate bulls, to replace heifers, and
to bring out the sick or injured cattle for treatment. The herd
instinct of cattle is tremendously strong, and to drive an individual cow and hold her against this tidal force, a horse must act
with knowledge, physical skill, and precision. Otherwise the cow
escapes and returns to a thoroughly upset herd.
—Thomas McGuane
Sugar

• • •

In the excitement of a stampede a man was not himself, and his horse was not the horse of yesterday. Man and horse were one, and the combination accomplished feats that would be utterly impossible under ordinary circumstances. Trained men can generally be found near the "point" at both sides of the herd. When the man on one side saw the herd bending his way he would fall back, and if the work were well done on the other side of the herd the stampede then gradually came to an end; the strain was removed, the cowboys were the happiest men on earth and their shouts and laughter could be heard for miles over the prairie.
—CHARLES GOODNIGHT
PROSE AND POETRY OF THE LIVE STOCK INDUSTRY

• • •

Always drink upstream from the herd.
—PROVERB

• • •

Following Chisholm's track became thousands of herds, and the trail became a very notable course. From 200 to 400 yards wide, beaten into the bare earth, it reached over hill and through valley for over 600 miles (including its southern extention), a chocolate band amid the green prairies, uniting the North and the South. As the marching hoofs wore it down and the wind blew and the waters washed the earth away, it became lower than the surrounding country and was flanked by little banks of sand, drifted by the wind.

—D. E. McARTHUR
THE CATTLE INDUSTRY OF TEXAS (1918)

• • •

Never drive black cattle at night.
—PROVERB

• • •

For every beast of the earth is mine, and the cattle upon a
thousand hills.
—*King James Bible*

• • •

The danger of swimming rivers is that the cattle set to milling,
and the first thing you know they will start to jump up and ride
on another, trying to climb out, and down they will go and you
will lose a lot of them. You have to keep them pointed for the
opposite bank, which means that in the water each man has to
hold his place alongside the herd, just lie on the trail.
—*Teddy Blue Abbot*

• • •

Cowards never lasted long enough to become real cowboys.
—CHARLES GOODNIGHT,
LEGENDARY CATTLEMAN

• • •

When you add it all up, the worst hardship we had on the trail was loss of sleep. Sometime we would rub tobacco juice in our eyes to keep awake.
—TEDDY BLUE ABBOT

• • •

If wishes were horses then beggars might ride.
—PROVERB

• • •

The bones of men and animals that lie bleaching along the trails abundantly testify that this was not the first instance in which the plain had baffled the determination of man.

—ANDY ADAMS
THE LOG OF A COWBOY

• • •

Loving was a man of religious instincts and one of the coolest and bravest men I have ever known, but devoid of caution.

—CHARLES GOODNIGHT,
LEGENDARY CATTLEMAN

• • •

Now a bull, or steer, is not difficult to dodge. He lowers his head, shuts his eyes, and comes on in one straight rush. But a cow looks to see what she is doing; her eyes are open every minute, and it overjoys her to take a side hook at you even when you succeed in eluding her direct charge.
—Stewart Edward White
The Drive

• • •

No harder life is lived by any working man. Our comfort was nothing; men were cheap, but cattle cost money.
—Andy Adams

• • •

Animals that have escaped for any length of time are almost as bad to handle as if they had never been broken.
—Theodore Roosevelt
The Round-Up

• • •

Before starting out on the trail, I made it a rule to draw up an article of agreement, setting forth what each man was to do. The main clause stipulated that if one shot another he was to be tried by the outfit and hanged on the spot, if found guilty. I never had a man shot on the trail.

—CHARLES GOODNIGHT,
LEGENDARY CATTLEMAN

• • •

As a rider guarding the herd he had never thought of the night's wildness and loneliness; as an outcast, now when the full silence set in, and the deep darkness, and the trains of radiant stars shone cold and calm, he lay with an ache in his heart.

—ZANE GREY
RIDERS OF THE PURPLE SAGE

• • •

And God said, let the earth bring forth the living creature after this kind, cattle and creeping things, the earth after his kind; and it was so.

—*KING JAMES BIBLE*

• • •

The method of work is simple. The mess-wagons and loose horses, after breaking camp in the morning, move on in a straight line for some few miles, going into camp again before midday; and the day herd, consisting of all the cattle that have been found far off their range, and which are to be brought back there, and of any others that it is necessary to gather, follows on afterwards.
—THEODORE ROOSEVELT
THE ROUND-UP

• • •

If you're riding point on the herd, every so often take a look over your shoulder, be sure they're still with you.
—UNKNOWN

• • •

All in all, my years on the trail were the happiest of my life. There were many hardships and dangers. Most of the time we were solitary adventurers in a great land as fresh and new as a spring morning, and we were free and full of the zest of dancers.
—CHARLES GOODNIGHT,
LEGENDARY CATTLEMAN

• • •

During the cattle drives, Texas cowboy music came into national significance. Its practical purpose is well known—it was used primarily to keep the herds quiet at night, for often a ballad sung loudly and continuously enough might prevent a stampede. However, the cowboy also sang because he liked to sing. . . . In this music of the range and trail is the grayness of the prairies, the mournful minor note of a Texas norther, and a rhythm that fits the gait of the cowboy's pony.
—ADMINISTRATION OF THE STATE OF TEXAS

• • •

This is the finest fence in the world. It's light as air, strong as whiskey, and cheaper than dirt!
—JOHN W. "BET-A-MILLION" GATES,
TEXAS BARBED WIRE SALESMAN

• • •

The trail's a lane, the trail's a lane
Dead is the branding fire.
The prairies wild are tame and mild,
All close corralled with wire.
—BADGER CLARK
THE PASSING OF THE TRAIL

• • •

PART 6

AROUND THE CAMPFIRE

The good Lord willing, and the creek don't rise.
—TRADITIONAL WESTERN SAYING

• • •

Here, if that hangin' rope didn't kill ya, maybe my coffee will.
—JUDGE FENTON
HANG 'EM HIGH
(1967)

• • •

There's no place around the campfire for a quitter's blanket.
—ANONYMOUS

• • •

"We been listenin' to your stories for fifteen years an' we don't
believe none of them."
"Well, why do you listen to 'em then?"
"'Cause we ain't got nothing else to do."
—*BONANZA*
(1969)

• • •

Call me anything you like, just don't call me late for supper.
—ANONYMOUS

• • •

It took all hands, and the cook.
—UNKNOWN

• • •

"Mounted on my favorite horse, my lariat near my hand, and my trusty guns in my belt . . . I felt I could defy the world."
—NAT "DEADWOOD DICK" LOVE

• • •

You can put your boots in the oven, but they won't come out biscuits.
—ANONYMOUS

• • •

"That was my kid brother that broke his arm. You did a good job, Doc, even if you were drunk."
"Thank you son. Professional compliments are always pleasing."
—RINGO KID AND DOC BOONE
STAGECOACH
(1939)

• • •

Remember to load your brain before shooting your mouth off.
—ANONYMOUS

• • •

The breakfast was speedily out of the way, and pipes were started
for a short smoke as the punchers walked over to the horse herd
to make their selections. By exercising patience, profanity and
perseverance they roped their hoses and saddled up.
—CLARANCE E.MULFORD
HOPALONG'S ROUND-UP

• • •

Never ask a man if he's from Texas. If he is, he'll
tell you on his own.
—UNKNOWN

• • •

The California I knew, old rancho California, is gone. It just doesn't exist, except maybe in little pockets. I live on the edge of the Mojave Desert, an area that used to be farm country. There were these fresh-produce stands with avocados and date palms. You could get a dozen artichokes for a buck or something. Totally wiped out now.
—SAM SHEPARD
THE PARIS REVIEW, SPRING 1997

• • •

Only a fool argues with the cook.
—ANONYMOUS

• • •

Are you sleeping or are you just checking for holes in your eye-lids?
—TRADITIONAL SMART CRACK

• • •

When a Texas cowboy was arrested for stealing a horse, he pleaded not guilty at his trial. When his lawyer managed to get him off and he was set free by the judge, he started to leave the courtroom. Suddenly he turned around and looked at the judge with puzzlement before asking, "Judge, does this mean I can keep the hoss?"
—UNKNOWN

• • •

Anything will taste good if you're hungry enough.
—ERIC "HOSS" CARTWRIGHT
BONANZA
(1963)

• • •

These men weren't vicious liars. It was love of romance, lack of reading matter, and the wish to be entertainin' that make 'em stretch facts and invent yarns. . . . This Babcock one night is telling about getting jumped by 50 hostile Sioux, a war party, that's giving him a close run. The bullets and arrows are tearin' the dirt all around, when he hits the mouth of a deep canyon. He thinks he's safe, but after ridin' up it a way, discovers it's a box gulch, with walls straight up from 600 to 1,000 feet. His only get-away's where he come in, an' the Indians are already whippin' their ponies into it.

Right here old Bab rares back in his chair, closes his eyes, and starts fondlin' his whiskers. This seems to be the end of the story, when one of his listeners asks:

"What happened then?"

Old Bab, with his eyes still closed, takin' a fresh chew, whispered: "They killed me, b'God!"

—CHARLES M. RUSSELL
SOME LIARS OF THE OLD WEST

• • •

To a cowboy, the difference between a good meal and a bad one
is the length of time between them.
—Unknown

• • •

I went to the wagon to get my roll,
To come back to Texas, dad-burn my soul.
—Traditional
The Old Chisholm Trail

• • •

I'm so hungry my belt buckle's rubbing a blister on my backbone.
—Unknown

• • •

Don't ever hit your mother with a shovel. It will leave a dull
impression on her mind.
—Attributed to Butch Cassidy

• • •

He's my boy. He's the best. Couldn't think more of him if he was
my own son.
—Gabby Hayes
(speaking about John Wayne)

• • •

I think you're going to find out that westerns will be coming
back. It's Americana, it's part of our history, the cowboy, the
cattle drive, the sheriff, the fight for law, order, and justice.
Justice will always prevail as far as I'm concerned.
—Clayton Moore

• • •

That there coffee'd melt a spoon!
—Traditional Cowboy Chuck Wagon Grumble

• • •

It sure is amusin' to read some of the old stories about cow-punchin'. You'd think a puncher growed horns an' was haired over. It put me in the mind of the eastern girl that asks her mother: "Ma," says she, "do cowboys eat grass?" "No, dear," says the old lady, "they're part human," an' I don't know but the old gal had 'em sized up right. If they are human, they're a separate species. I'm talkin' about the old-time ones, before the country's strung with wire an' nesters had grabbed all the water, a' a cow-puncher's home was big. It wasn't where he took his hat off, but where he spread his blankets."
—Rawhide Rawlins,
The Story of the Cowpuncher
by Charles M. Russell

• • •

If he'd a gone any slower, he'd hafta go backward just to keep
moving.
—TRADITIONAL

• • •

If there's anything I don't like, it's driving a stagecoach through
Apache country.
—BUCK
STAGECOACH
(1939)

• • •

Bean was the proprietor of the Jersey Lily tavern in Langtry, Texas, close to the railroad. One day when a train stopped to take on water, a passenger rushed into Bean's bar for a bottle of beer. Bean lazily told him to help himself, which the man did, rushing out again without paying. Incensed, Bean grabbed his gun and ran up to the train, telling the conductor to hold it; he found the customer in the smoking car and, cocking his gun, demanded money for the beer. Alarmed, the man handed over a ten dollar bill. Bean took it and said, "Fifty cents for the beer, nine dollars and fifty cents for collecting. This squares your account. You can keep the bottle." Then stepping down from the train he told the conductor, "You can go ahead now as soon as you damn well please."
—Unknown

• • •

"Who's that you just asked about?"
"Hoppy . . . Hopalong Cassidy."
"Kinda out of his territory, ain't he?"
"I wouldn't say that. Anywhere you find Hoppy—
that's his territory."
—*Hop-a-long Cassidy*
(1935)

• • •

There were two round-ups each year. The siring round-up was the more important, and was called the "calf round-up" because it was then the calves were branded. The fall round-up caught the summer calves and strays that the first one had missed.
—Walter Prescott Webb
The Cattle Kingdom

• • •

B-r-r! I'm sleepy. Lets go by-by. Wake that dern Mexican up and
make him keep watch till the sheriff comes!
—EUGENE MANLOVE RHODES
THE TROUBLE MAN

• • •

The big house will be down by the river and the corrals and the
barns behind it. It'll be a good place to live in. Ten years and I'll
have the Red River "D" on more cattle than you've looked at
anywhere. I'll have that brand on enough beef to feed the whole
country. Good beef for hungry people. Beef to make 'em strong
and make 'em grow. But it takes work and it takes sweat and it
takes time. Lots of time. It takes years.
—TOM DUNSON
RED RIVER
(1948)

• • •

"But Pecos Bill found a cheaper way of makin' post holes."

"What was his new method?" asked Lanky.

"Why he jest went out and rounded up a big bunch of prairie-dogs, and turned 'em loose where he wanted the fence, and of course every critter of 'em begun diggin' a hole, for it's jest prairie-dog nature to dig holes. As soon as a prairie-dog would git down about two feet, Bill would yank him out and stick a post in the hole. Then the fool prairie-dog would go start another one, and Bill would git it. Bill said he found prairie-dog labor very satisfactory. The only trouble was that sometimes durin' off hours, the badgers that he had gradin' would make a raid on the prairie-dogs, and Bill would have to git up and drive 'em back to their own camp."

—Mody C. Boatright and Lanky

Pecos Bill

• • •

PART 7

COWBOY LOVE

"Did you ever think about getting married again?
"Oh, I think about it; never in daylight."
—Roslyn (Marilyn Monroe) to Gay (Clark Gable)
The Misfits
(1961)

• • •

There has to be a woman, but not much of one. A good horse is
much more important.
—Max Brand, on writing westerns

• • •

Women! I never met one yet that was half as reliable as a horse.
—JOHN WAYNE

• • •

There were only two things the old-time cowpunchers were
afraid of: a decent woman and being set afoot.
—E.C. "TEDDY BLUE" ABBOTT

• • •

Happy as a rooster in a henhouse.
—UNKNOWN

• • •

There are always women who will take men on their own terms.
If I were a man I wouldn't bother to change while there are
women like that around.
—ANNIE OAKLEY

• • •

"Gene, *(pointing to his gunbelt)* I'll take . . . "
"All right, sheriff . . . I know."
"The ladies say they're not comfortable to dance with."
—Gene Autry surrenders his six-shooter on
entering the dancehall
The Gene Autry Show
(1950)

• • •

Cowboys are like outhouses, all the best ones are taken.
—Anonymous

• • •

"Three weeks ago I took a bullet out of a man who was shot by a
gentleman. The bullet was in his back!"
—Hatfield to Doc Boone
Stagecoach
(1939)

• • •

You know you have the keys to a cowboy's heart when he lets you ride his horse.
—ANONYMOUS

• • •

"Hadn't you better introduce me to your friend?"
"Do you mean you don't know me? Why I'm Jerry, Janet's little sister!"
"The little freckle-faced kid that could never keep her stockings up?"
"Uh-huh."
"I can't believe it! I do't know whether to kiss you or spank you."
"Don't you think I'm a little old to be spanked?"
"I suppose you are. And it's probably a little too public to, ah, well anyway, it's too public."
—GENE AUTRY
TUMBLING TUMBLEWEEDS
(1935)

• • •

If you can rope me, you can have me.
—Unknown

• • •

"Please take me with you. I'm strong. I can stand
anything you can."
"It's too much for a woman."
"Too much for a woman? Put your arms around me, Tom. (*They
hug and kiss.*) Hold me, feel me in your arms. Do I feel weak,
Tom? I don't, do I? Oh, you'll need me. You'll need a woman.
You'll need what a woman can give you to do what you have to
do. Oh, listen to me, Tom. Listen with your head and your heart
too. The sun only shines half the time, Tom. The other half is
night."
"I've made up my mind."
"Oh, change your mind, Tom. Just once in your life, change your
mind."
"I'll send for ya. Will ya come?"
"Of course I'll come. But you're wrong."
—Fen and Tom Dunson
Red River
(1948)

• • •

Cowboys weren't allowed to kiss girls in pictures, so one time I gave Dale a little peck on the forehead and we got a ton of letters to leave that mushy stuff out . . . so I had to kiss Trigger instead.
—ROY ROGERS

• • •

Cowboys ain't easy to love, and they're harder to hold."
—WILLIE NELSON

• • •

"Gabby, I thought you hated all women."
"Nope, just the uppity ones."
—GABBY HAYES
BORDERTOWN GUN FIGHTERS
(1943)

• • •

You can't get a man with a gun, that's for sure!
—ANNIE OAKLEY

• • •

"Pa told you to keep an eye on me? What in heck for?"
"To keep you from getting' chsed all the way back to the Pon-
derosa by some hoppin' mad daddy with a shotgun in his
hand . . . and from the look in your eye that's just about what's
gonna happen."
—ERIC "HOSS" CARTWRIGHT AND JOSEPH "LITTLE JOE"
CARTWRIGHT
BONANZA
(1961)

• • •

So many cowboys, so little rope.
—ANONYMOUS

• • •

"String wire? I'm sorry Gene, but I'm workin' on something else."
"Blonde or redhead?
"See for yourself."
"Not bad. I'd like to meet her myself."
"So would I."
—*TWILIGHT ON THE RIO GRANDE*
(1947)

• • •

There's two theories to arguing with a woman.
Neither of them works.
—WILL ROGERS

• • •

The lovers parted with a long embrace. "You are not going too?" said the Duchess, as she saw Mr. Oakhurst apparently waiting to accompany him. "As far as the canyon," he replied. He turned suddenly and kissed the Duchess, leaving her pallid face aflame, and her trembling limbs rigid with amazement.
—BRET HARTE
THE OUTCASTS OF POKER FLAT

• • •

"You're looking pretty tonight, Kitty."
"How is it you never tell me that in the daytime?"
—MARSHAL MATT DILLON AND KITTY RUSSELL
GUNSMOKE

• • •

Folks, if you're as tired of listening to your favorite commentator
as I am, you'll be glad to know that this is her last broadcast.
From now on she'll do her broadcasting from the kitchen, 'cause
I'm going to marry her.
—GENE AUTRY
ROVING TUMBLEWEEDS
(1939)

● ● ●

Save money on the bull, ride a cowboy instead.
—ANONYMOUS

● ● ●

The older the guitar, the sweeter the music.
—PROVERB

● ● ●

Love is dope, not chicken soup.
—TOM ROBBINS
EVEN COWGIRLS GET THE BLUES

● ● ●

I wish I could find words to express the trueness, the bravery, the
hardihood, the sense of honor, the loyalty to their trust and to
each other of the old trail hands.
—CHARLES GOODNIGHT,
LEGENDARY CATTLEMAN

● ● ●

Love of man for woman—love of woman for man. That's the
nature, the meaning, the best of life itself.
—ZANE GREY
RIDERS OF THE PURPLE SAGE

● ● ●

"I don't blame you for running away after you didn't answer my letters. All is forgiven. You look the same, except for the frown. How come you stopped writing anyway?"
"Well, you see, I didn't think it was just right to go on after I . . . "
(She indicates her wedding ring)
—*TUMBLING TUMBLEWEEDS*
(1935)

• • •

C'mon Little Joe, she's not for you. Stuff your eyes back into your head, they're about to pop out.
—ERIC "HOSS" CARTWRIGHT TO JOSEPH "LITTLE JOE" CARTWRIGHT
BONANZA (1959)

• • •

A man never knows what true happiness is until he gets married—and then it's too late.
—*THE GENE AUTRY SHOW*
"A NARROW ESCAPE"
(1953)

• • •

I have fallen in love with American names,
The sharpe names that never get fat,
The snakeskin titles of mining claims,
The plumed war-bonnet of Medicine Hat,
Tucson and Deadwood and Lost Mule Flat.
—STEPHEN VINCENT BENET
AMERICAN NAMES

• • •

The only good reason to ride a bull is to meet a nurse.
—UNKNOWN

• • •

"Look, Miss Dalls. You no folks . . . neither have I, and, well,
maybe I'm takin' a lot for granted but . . . I watched you with that
baby—that other woman's baby. You looked . . . well, well I still
got a ranch across the border. There's a nice place—a real nice
place . . . trees . . . grass . . . water. There's a cabin half built. A man
could live there . . . and a woman. Will you go?"
"But you don't know me."
"I know all I wanna know. Will you go?"
—RINGO KID TO DALLLAS
STAGECOACH
(1939)

• • •

PART 8

COWBOY PHILOSOPHY

So we mostly size a fellow up by his abilities as a trouble man.
Any kind of trouble—not necessarily the fightin' kind. If he goes
the route, if he sets to the limit, if he's enlisted for the war—why,
you most naturally depend on him.
—Eugene Manlove Rhodes
The Trouble Man

• • •

Don't let the grit in your boots keep you from walking tall.
—Traditional Cowboy Saying

• • •

You can wash your hands but not your conscience.
—PROVERB

• • •

Well, there are some things a man just can't run away from.
—RINGO KID
STAGECOACH
(1939)

• • •

If it don't seem worth the effort, it probably ain't.
—ANONYMOUS

• • •

Life's a whole lot simpler if you plow around the stump.
—Proverb

• • •

Well I don't favor talking to vermin, but I'll talk to you this once.
—John Chisum to Lawrence Murphy
(Their feud grew into what became known as the
"Lincoln County War.")

• • •

The quickest way to double your money is to put it back in your jeans.
—Proverb

• • •

Every man's got to fight his own battle in his own way.
—ERIC "HOSS" CARTWRIGHT
BONANZA
(1963)

• • •

Time's precious, so waste it wisely.
—UNKNOWN

• • •

It's immoral to let a sucker keep his money.
—"CANADA BILL" JONES,
CARDSHARP OF THE 1800S

• • •

Think before you open your mouth. Look before you take a step.
—ANONYMOUS

• • •

You cannot weigh the facts accurately if you got the scales
weighed down with your own opinions.
—PROVERB

• • •

Hate? Isn't that a strong word to use just because you don't agree
with someone?
—LUCAS MCCAIN
THE RIFLEMAN
(1960)

• • •

Whichever way your luck is running, it's bound to change.
—Proverb

• • •

Judge Roy Bean was said to conduct marriages for $5 and divorces for $10. When he was informed that he surely did have the authority to conduct marriages but could not grant divorces, the Judge reposted, "I have the right to undo any wrong I have done."
—Traditional Western Anecdote

• • •

If it's true that honesty is the best policy, how come folks get so mad when you tell them the truth about themselves?
—Anonymous

• • •

Most men are more afraid of being thought cowards than of anything else, and a lot more afraid of being thought physical cowards than moral ones.
—WALTER VAN TILBURG CLARK
THE OX-BOW INCIDENT (1943)

• • •

Never follow good whiskey with water, lessen you're out of good whiskey.
—UNKNOWN

• • •

Keep your eye on the high mark and you will hit it. Not the first time nor the second and maybe not the third, but if you keep on aiming and keep on trying, you'll hit the bull's eye of success.
—ANNIE OAKLEY

• • •

There's nothing you can do to keep trouble from visiting, but you don't have to offer it a chair.
—UNKNOWN

• • •

What this country needs is dirtier fingernails and cleaner minds.
—WILL ROGERS

• • •

Whiskey sure is a brave-maker, and if a man had enough of this booze you couldn't drown him. You could even shoot a man through the brain or heart and he wouldn't die till he sobered up.
—CHARLES M. RUSSELL
WHISKEY

• • •

Coolness and a steady nerve will always beat simple quickness.
—PROVERB

• • •

You know, sometimes when a person don't know what to do, the
best thing is to just stand still.
—GAY (CLARK GABLE)
THE MISFITS
(1961)

• • •

Timing has a lot to do with the outcome of a rain dance.
—PROVERB

• • •

Poker is a science: the highest court in Texas has said so.
—QUINCE FORREST
ANDY ADAMS,
THE LOG OF A COWBOY

• • •

Love your enemies, but keep your six-gun handy.
—UNKNOWN

• • •

Think what you please, the Kid had a lot of principle. He was about as honest a fellow as I ever knew outside of some loose notions about rustling cattle."
—FRANK COE
ON BILLY THE KID

• • •

Don't take a very big person to carry a grudge.
—ANONYMOUS

• • •

Lord . . . whatever I've done to piss you off . . . if you could just get me out of this and somehow let me know what it was I promise to rectify the situation.
—*MAVERICK*
(1994)

• • •

God intended women to be outside as well as men, and they do not know what they are missing when they stay cooped up in the house with a novel.
—ANNIE OAKLEY

• • •

Never wake a sleeping rattler.
—UNKNOWN

• • •

No matter where people go, sooner or later there's the law. And sooner or later they find God's already been there.
—JOHN CHISUM
CHISUM
(1970)

• • •

Talk slowly, think quickly.
—PROVERB

• • •

A man doesn't run from a fight, Mark . . . but that doesn't mean
you should go running *to one* either.
—LUCAS MCCAIN
THE RIFLEMAN
(1961)

• • •

We're not nearly as violent as the westerns.
—MOE HOWARD OF THE THREE STOOGES

• • •

"If I deputized an escaped convict. I'd be run outta the territory."
"It's better'n being carried out."
—MARSHAL WILCOX AND RINGO KID
STAGECOACH
(1986)

• • •

The worst troublemaker you're ever likely to meet watches you
shave his face in the mirror every morning.
—UNKNOWN

• • •

A shadow only means that there's shining somewhere.
—PROVERB

• • •

Folks around here judge a man by what he is, not what he was.
—BEN CARTWRIGHT
BONANZA
(1963)

• • •

"Tell Don Diego, tell him that all the land north of that river's mine. Tell him to stay off of it."

"Oh, but the land is his."

"Where did he get it from?"

"Oh many years ago by grant and patent, inscribed by the King of Spain."

"You mean he took it away from whomever was here before. Indians maybe?"

"Maybe so."

"Well, I'm takin' it away from him."

—TOM DUNSON AND DON DIEGO'S HIRED KILLER
RED RIVER
(1948)

• • •

Good judgment comes from experience, and a lot of that comes
from bad judgment.
—UNKNOWN

• • •

You really don't believe in political solutions do you?
—SISSY
EVEN COWGIRLS GET THE BLUES BY TOM ROBBINS

• • •

If lawyers are dis-barred, and clerics are de-frocked, shouldn't it
follow that cowboys are de-ranged?
—ANONYMOUS

• • •

Sometimes the cowboys off duty will go to town late in the evening and there join with some party of cowboys—whose herd is sold and they preparing to start home—in having a jolly time. Often one or more of them will imbibe too much poison whisky and straightaway go on the "war path." Then mounting his pony he is ready to shoot anybody or anything; or rather than not shoot at all, would fire up into the air, all the while yelling as only a semi-civilized being can. At such times it is not safe to be on the streets, or for that matter within a house, for the drunk cowboy would as soon shoot into a house as at anything else.

—JOSEPH G. MCCOY
ABILENE IN 1868

• • •

You can't go hunting men like coyotes after rabbits and not feel anything about it. Not without being like any other animal. The worst animal.

—WALTER VAN TILBURG CLARK
THE OX-BOW INCIDENT (1943)

• • •

Men are the enemies of women, promising sublime intimacy, unequalled passion, amazing security, and grace. They nevertheless exploit and injure in a myriad of subtle ways. Without men the world would be a better place: softer, kinder, more loving; calmer, quieter, more humane.
—ANNIE OAKLEY

• • •

If you find yourself in a hole, for Lord's sakes, stop digging!
—TRADITIONAL WESTERN SAYING

• • •

"You and your education!"
"Education is progress! What have you got against it?"
"I don't have anything against education—as long as it doesn't interfere with your thinking!"
—BEN CARTWRIGHT AND ADAM CARTWRIGHT
BONANZA
(1959)

• • •

Never take down another man's fence.
—UNKNOWN

• • •

A man raised amidst the hardships and privations of a rough frontier life knows how to look for Nature for relief. Sometimes hot water is best; sometimes cold water serves the purpose.
—H. H. HALSELL
THE TRUE COWBOY

• • •

Which would you rather have? What's behind, or what might be ahead?
—MATT GARTH
RED RIVER
(1948)

• • •

COWBOY, n: A man with guts and a horse.
URBAN COWBOY, n: One who is typically all hat and no cow.
—THE COWBOY DICTIONARY

• • •

I found him a loyal friend and good company. He was a dentist whom necessity had made a gambler; a gentleman whom disease had made a vagabond; a philosopher whom life had made a caustic wit; a long, lean, blonde fellow, nearly dead with consumption and at the same time the most skillful gambler and nerviest speediest, deadliest man with a six-gun I ever knew.
—WYATT EARP
ABOUT DOC HOLLIDAY

• • •

"Ol' Pat . . . Sheriff Pat Garrett. Sold out to the Santa Fe ring. How does it feel?"
"It feels like . . . times have changed."
"Times, maybe. Not me."
—BILLY THE KID AND PAT GARRETT
PAT GARRETT AND BILLY THE KID
(1973)

• • •

Death Sentence, 1881

Jose Manuel Miguel Xaviar Gonzales, in a few short weeks, it will be spring, the snows of winter will flee away, the ice will vanish, and the air will become soft and balmy, in short, Jose Miguel Xaviar Gonzales, the annual miracle of the years will awaken and come to pass, but you won't be there.

The rivulet will run its soaring course to the sea, the timid desert flowers will put forth their tender shoots, the glorious valleys of this imperial domain will blossom as the rose, still you won't be here to see.

From every tree top some wild woods songster will carol his mating song, butterflies will sport in the sunshine, the busy bee will hum, happy as it pursues its accustomed vocation. The gentle breeze will tease the tassels of the wild grasses, and all nature, Jose Manuel Miguel Xaviar Gonzales, will be glad, but you, you won't be here to enjoy it because I command the sheriff or some other officers of the country to lead you out to some remote spot, wring you by the neck from a knotting bough of some sturdy oak; and let you hang until you are dead.

And then, Jose Manuel Miguel Xaviar Gonzales, I further command that such officer or officers retire quickly from your dangling corpse, that vultures may descend from the heavens upon your filthy body until nothing shall remain but bare, bleached bones of a cold-blooded, copper-colored, blood-thirsty, throat- cutting, chili-eating, sheep-herding, murdering son-of-a-bitch.

—HONORABLE JUDGE ROY BEAN
UNITED STATES OF AMERICA V. GONZALES (1881)

• • •

To live fully, one must be free, but to be free one must give up security. Therefore, to live one must be ready to die. How's that for a paradox?
—Tom Robbins
Even Cowgirls Get the Blues

• • •

"I wouldn't mind going broke so much," said Dick Mason, "but I sure hate to see the cattle die, and me not able to do the first thing to save them."
—Eugene Manlove Rhodes
Aforesaid Bates

• • •

Live yourself a good honest life. Then when you grow older you can look back and enjoy it a second time.
—Proverb

• • •

I have vision. The rest of the world wears bi-focals.
—BUTCH CASSIDY

• • •

Other times he could not afford to eat. But there was never a day when he wanted to trade his chaps for a job with a boss looking over his shoulder.
—DIRK JOHNSON
A COWBOY'S LAST CHANCE

• • •

"Goin' somewhere?"
"Isn't everybody?"
—BEN CARTWRIGHT AND ERIC "HOSS" CARTWRIGHT
BONANZA
(1963)

• • •

Never shoot an unarmed or unwarned enemy. This may be called the "rattlesnake code": always warn before you strike.
—DUBIOUS COWBOY WISDOM

• • •

A pioneer is a man who turned all the grass upside down, strung bob-wire over the dust that was left, poisoned the water, cut down the trees, killed the Indian who owned the land and called it progress
—CHARLES M. RUSSELL

• • •

During his time as a rancher, Roosevelt and one of his cow-punchers, riding over the range, lassoed a maverick, a two-year-old steer that had never been branded. They lit a fire then and there and prepared the branding irons. The part of the range they were on was claimed by Gregor Lang, one of Roosevelt's neighbors. According to the rule among cattlemen the steer therefore belonged to Lang, having been found on his land. As the cowboy applied the brand, Roosevelt said, "Wait, it should be Lang's brand, a thistle."

"That's alright boss," said the cowboy, continuing to apply the brand.

"But you're putting on my brand."

"That's right," said the man, "I always put on the boss's brand."

"Drop that iron," said Roosevelt, "and get back to the ranch and get out. I don't need you anymore."

The cowboy protested, but Roosevelt was adamant. "A man who will steal *for* me will steal *from* me," he declared. So the cowboy went, and the story spread all over the Badlands.

—Unknown

• • •

Most new booze is worse than trade whiskey. Whiskey made all men brave. If nobody got drunk the East Coast would be awful crowded by this time. Maybe the leaders of the exploring party didn't drink, but the men that went with them did. It's a safe bet there wasn't a man in Columbus' crew that knowed what a maple-nut sundae was.
—CHARLES M. RUSSELL
WHISKEY

• • •

On the Southwestern Cattleman:

They are, as a class, not public spirited in matters pertaining to the general good, but may justly be called selfish, or at least indifferent to the public welfare. They are prodigal to a fault with their money, when opportunity offers to gratify their appetites or passions, but it is extremely difficult to induce them to expend even a small sum in forwarding a project or enterprise that has other than a purely selfish end in view. In general they entertain strong suspicions of Northern men, and do not have the profoundest confidence in each other. They are disposed to measure every man's action and prompting motives by the rule of selfishness, and they are slow indeed to believe that other than purely selfish motives could or ever do prompt a man to do an act or develop an enterprise.

—Joseph G. McCoy
Abilene in 1868

• • •

I must say that the "cow-punchers" as a class, maligned and traduced as they have been, possess a quality of sturdy sterling manhood which would be to the credit of men in any walk of life. The honor of the average "puncher" abides with him continually. He will not lie; he will not steal. He keeps faith with his friends; toward his enemies he bears himself like a man. He has vices—as who has not?—but I like to speak softly of them when set against his unassailable virtues. I wish that the manhood of the cowboy might come into fashion further East.

—Frederic Remington
Life in the Cattle Country

• • •

Whiskey has been blamed for lots it didn't do. It's a brave-maker. All men know it. If you want to know a man, get him drunk and he'll tip his hand. If I like a man when I'm sober, I kin hardly keep from kissing him when I'm drunk. This goes both ways. If I don't like a man when I'm sober, I don't want him in the same town when I'm drunk.

—Charles M. Russell
Whiskey

• • •

With the march of progress came the railroad, and no longer were we called upon to follow the long-horned steers, or mustangs on the trail, while the immense cattle ranges, stretching away in the distance as far as the eye could see, now began to be dotted with cities and towns and the cattle industry, which once held a monopoly in the West, now had to give way to the industry of the farm and the mill. To us wild cowboys of the range, used to the wild and unrestricted life of the boundless plains, the new order of things did not appeal, and many of us became disgusted and quit the wild life for the pursuits of our more civilized brother. I was among that number and in 1890 I bid farewell to the life which I had followed for over twenty years.
—NAT "DEADWOOD DICK" LOVE

• • •

When a man knows something, he really knows—deep down in his heart—he doesn't have to prove it or argue—just knowing is enough.
—BEN CARTWRIGHT
BONANZA
(1963)

• • •

PART 9

COWBOY STUFF

Mr. Moore had got his cowboy training in California, where they use "Center-fire," high horn saddles and riatas, (ropes) which they wrap around the saddle-horn when roping on horseback. The cinches on these saddles being broad, and in the center of the saddle, which makes it difficult to keep the saddle right on the pony's back. He had persuaded many of his cowboys to use these saddles and the long rawhide riatas—hence a large order had been sent to California in the early spring. I sent for one of these ten dollar bridle bits, and am still using it to ride with.
—CHARLES SIRINGO
AN ELEVEN HUNDRED MILE RIDE DOWN THE CHISHOLM TRAIL

• • •

The cowboy's outfit of clothing, as a rule, is one of the best from hat to boots, he may not have a dollar in the world, but he will wear good, substantial clothing, even if he has to buy it on credit, and he usually has plenty of that. I once heard a minister in a little Northern town, in using the cowboy as an illustration, say "The Cowboy with an eighteen dollar hat and a two dollar suit of clothing is as happy as a king on his throne." In fact, extravagance is one of the cowboy's failings.

—W. S. JAMES
STYLE ON THE RANCH

• • •

Nothing fits better than old boots, old jeans, and an old hat.
—ANONYMOUS

• • •

Always uses top grade hemp, Schmidt does. He oils it so it slided real good. Snaps your neck like a dry twig.
—*HANG 'EM HIGH*
(1968)

• • •

Above all things, the plainsmen had to have in instinct for direction. I never had a compass in my life, but I was never lost.
—CHARLES GOODNIGHT,
LEGENDARY CATTLEMAN

• • •

In the times when some men needed guns and all men carried them, no pistol of less than .44-caliber was tolerated on the range; the solid framed .45-caliber being the one almost universally used. The barrel was eight inches long, and it shot a rifle cartridge of forty grains of powder and a blunt-ended missile. This weapon depended from a belt worn loose resting upon the left hip and hanging low down on the right hip so that none of the weight came upon the abdomen. This was typical, for the cowboy was neither fancy gunmen nor army officer. The latter carries the revolver on the left, the butt pointing forward.
—EMERSON HOUGH
THE COWBOY

• • •

Don't spill none of that liquor, son. It eats right into the bar.
—*The Over the Hill Gang*
(1969)

• • •

They paid us off, and I bought some new clothes and got my picture taken. I had a new white Stetson hat that I paid ten dollars for and new pants that cost twelve dollars, and a good shirt and fancy boots. Lord, was I proud of those clothes! When my sister saw me she said, "Take your pants out of your boots and put your coat on. You look like an outlaw." I told her to go to hell. And I never did like her after that.
—E.C. "Teddy Blue" Abbott

• • •

May your belly never grumble.
May your heart never ache.
May your horse never stumble.
May your cinch never break.
—Traditional Western Saying

• • •

A cowboy was not educated, but he received lessons from contact
with Nature and the hardships of life which qualified him to
think for himself and know how to measure men by correct
standards. He was laconic in speech, using few words to express
himself, but his meanings were forceful and easily understood
by his comrades. He wore serviceable Stetson hats, shop-made
boots, costly overshirts and usually a silk handkerchief around
his neck. The real old-time cowboy of my time never went
gaudily dressed as they now do in the picture-shows.
—H. H. HALSELL
THE TRUE COWBOY

• • •

Cowpunchers were mighty particular about their rig, an' in all
the camps you'd find a fashion leader. From a cowpuncher's idea,
these fellers was sure good to look at, an' I tell you right now,
there ain't no prettier sight for my eyes than one of those good-
lookin', long-backed cowpunchers, sittin' up on a high-forked,
full-stamped California saddle with a live hoss between his legs.
—RAWHIDE RAWLINS,
THE STORY OF THE COWPUNCHER BY CHARLES M. RUSSELL

• • •

A long time ago, I learned something about this big wide open
West of ours. You know, when a man rides out here he feels
bigger himself. He sort of Grows up—expands like the country
around him.
—*THE GENE AUTRY SHOW*
"SADDLE UP" (1955)

• • •

It doesn't matter how big a ranch you have, or how many cattle
you brand, or how many dollars you have, the size of your funeral
is still going to depend on the weather.
—UNKNOWN

• • •

Oh, a ten-dollar hoss and a forty-dollar saddle,
And I'm goin' to punchin' Texas cattle.
—TRADITIONAL
THE OLD CHISHOLM TRAIL

• • •

Sometimes the demands were so urgent that a man's boots would not be taken off his feet for an entire week. The nerves of the men usually became wrought up to such a tension that no man was to be touched by another when he was asleep until after he had been spoken to. The man who suddenly aroused a sleeper was liable to be shot, as all were thoroughly armed and understood the instant use of the revolver or the rifle.

—Charles Goodnight
Prose and Poetry of the Live Stock Industry

• • •

The wagon outfit consists of the "Chuck Wagon" which carries the food bedding and tents, and from the back of which the food is prepared over an open fire. The "Hoodlum Wagon," which carries the water barrel, wood and branding irons, furnishes the Chuck Wagon with water and wood, the branding crew with wood, and attends all round-ups or branding pens with a supply of drinking water.

—Walter Prescott Webb
The Great Plains (1931)

• • •

The cowboy's boots were of fine leather and fitted tightly, with light narrow soles, extremely small and high heels. Surely a more irrational foot-covering never was invented; yet these tight, peaked cowboy boots had a great significance and may indeed be called the insignia of a calling. There was no prouder soul on earth than the cowboy. He was proud of being a horseman and had a contempt for all human beings who walked. On foot in his tight-toed boots he was lost; but he wished it to be understood that he never was on foot.
—EMERSON HOUGH
THE COWBOY

• • •

During the war his clothing was made from homespun cloth, he had no other, home-made shoes or boots, even his hat was home-made, the favorate hat material being straw. Rye straw was the best. Sometime a fellow would get hold of a Mexican hat, and then he was sailing.
—W. S. JAMES
STYLE ON THE RANCH

• • •

Every cowboy furnishes his own saddle bridle, saddle blanket, and spurs; also his bedding, known as a "Hot Roll," a 16 to 20 oz. canvas "Tarp" about 18 feet long doubled and bedding in between, usually composed of several quilts known as "suggans" and blankets—rarely a mattress, the extra quilts serving for mattress. The top "Tarp" serves as extra covering and protects against rain.

—FRANK S. HASTINGS
SOME GLIMPSES INTO RANCH LIFE

• • •

PART 10

ONE-LINERS

I wanted someone to kill me, so concluded to go to the Black
Hills.
—CHARLES SIRINGO

• • •

Careful as a naked man climbing a barb wire fence.
—UNKNOWN

• • •

Meaner than a gut-shot grizzly.
—TRADITIONAL WESTERN SAYING

• • •

The emptier the barrel, the louder the noise.
—ANONYMOUS

• • •

The only sure thing about luck is that it will change.
—BRET HARTE

• • •

A man that straddles a fence usually has a sore crotch.
—ANONYMOUS

• • •

Let's just live.
—Gay (Clark Gable)
The Misfits (1961)

• • •

Telling a fella to get lost is a whole lot different than making him
do it.
—Anonymous

• • •

Conform and be dull.
—J. Frank Dobie
The Voice of the Coyote

• • •

He's all right. He went through that wall head first.
—UNKNOWN

• • •

You can always tell a cowboy, but you can't tell him much.
—UNKNOWN

• • •

Mad as a mule chewin' bumblebees.
—ANONYMOUS

• • •

My forefathers didn't come over on the *Mayflower*, but they met
the boat.
—WILL ROGERS

• • •

Should you get to thinking that you're a person of some influence, try ordering someone else's dog around.
—Anonymous

• • •

Courage! It's easy to have courage with a gun in your hand.
—Anonymous

• • •

Grab what you can and let the loose ends drag.
—Anonymous

• • •

That man could talk the hinges off a gate!
—Anonymous

• • •

Never expect a handout, and never wait for anyone to hand you anything.
—JESSE JAMES

• • •

To learn what money is worth, try borrowing some.
—UNKNOWN

• • •

The last time that bear ate a lawyer, he had the runs for thirty-three days.
—PAUL NEWMAN AS ROY BEAN
(REFERRING TO THE BEAR BEAN HAD CHAINED OUTSIDE OF HIS PLACE.)
THE LIFE AND TIMES OF JUDGE ROY BEAN
(1972)

• • •

You can't get lard 'less you boil the pig.
—UNKNOWN

• • •

We'll use a signal I have tried and found far-reaching and easy to yell. Waa-hoo!
—ZANE GREY
THE LAST OF THE PLAINSMEN

• • •

Cowboys don't never bathe, they just dust off.
—ANONYMOUS

• • •

He's plumb soap-and-water crazy, so damn clean that he's dirty.
—BOB KENNON
SOME COOKS I HAVE KNOWN

• • •

It is easier to get an actor to be a cowboy then to get a cowboy to
be an actor.
—JOHN FORD

• • •

I didn't have the guts to be a cowboy. I had the ignorance.
—UNKNOWN

• • •

Game? I was born game, Sis, and hope to die in that condition.
—*ROOSTER COCKBURN*
TRUE GRIT BY CHARLES PORTIS

• • •

I take no sass but sassparilla.
—ATTRIBUTED TO JOHN WESLEY HARDIN

• • •

It'll feel a whole lot better, so as it quits hurtin'.
—UNKNOWN

• • •

Deader than a can of Spam.
—TRADITIONAL WESTERN SAYING

• • •

A bird in the hand is a certainty. But a bird in the bush may sing.
—BRET HARTE

• • •

Is that a man or a horse?
—UNKNOWN

• • •

Don't sell your mule to buy a plow.
—PROVERB

• • •

Young Whipper Snapper!
—GABBY HAYES

• • •

Hey, go in there and get me a bottle of whiskey to keep me
primed for the rodeo.
—PERCE (MONTGOMERY CLIFT)
THE MISFITS
(1961)

• • •

Six of one, or a half dozen of the other.
—ANONYMOUS

• • •

Courage is being scared to death, and saddling up anyway.
—JOHN WAYNE

• • •

A cow-chip is paradise for a fly.
—UNKNOWN

• • •

Never ask a barber if he thinks you need a haircut
—PROVERB

• • •

If you are going to kill time, work it to death.
—PROVERB

• • •

For me, sitting still is harder than any kind of work.
—ANNIE OAKLEY

• • •

They'll have to shoot me first to take my gun.
—ROY ROGERS

• • •

Out West you lived a long time. Even horse thieves had to hang
five minutes longer than anywhere else.
—PROVERB

• • •

Before cussin' the boss, saddle your hoss.
—ANONYMOUS

• • •

Every tub stands on its own bottom.
—JOHN WESLEY HARDIN

• • •

You can't get down gracefully if you're riding a high-horse.
—PROVERB

• • •

Hang 'em first, try 'em later.
—ROY BEAN

• • •

Behind every successful rancher is a wife who works in town.
—UNKNOWN

• • •

If you refer to your spurs as "the family silver," you might be a cowboy.
—ANONYMOUS

• • •

You might be a cowboy if your favorite fragrance is "leather."
—UNKNOWN

• • •

You don't learn much when everything goes right.
—PROVERB

• • •

You can never step in the same river twice.
—PROVERB

• • •

In 1890 the United States Census Bureau declared that the
American frontier had come to an end.
—EDITOR

• • •

Here's to the sunny slopes of long ago.
—AUGUSTUS MCCRAE
LONESOME DOVE BY LARRY MCMURTRY

• • •

There's tall grass yet. Tall hay—cured on the stem.
—BATES
EUGENE MANLOVE RHODES,
AFORESAID BATES

• • •

Yer durn tootin'!
—GABBY HAYES

PART 11

• • •

THE DYING COWBOY

"O bury me not on the lone prairie,"
These words came low and mournfully
From the pallid lips of a youth who lay
On his dying couch at the close of day.
He had wailed in pain till o'er his brow
Death's shadows fast were gathering now;
He thought of his home nd his loved one nigh
As the cowboys gathered to see him die.
"It matters not, I've oft been told
Where the body lies when the heart grows cold;
Yet grant, O grant, this wish to me,
O bury me not on the lone prairie.
O bury me not on the lone prairie
Where the wild coyotes will howl over me,
In a narrow grave just six by three,
O bury me not on the lone prairie.
"O bury me not," and his voice failed there,
But we took no heed of his dying prayer;
In a narrow grave just six by three
We buried him there on the lone prairie.

—TRADITIONAL

• • •

INDEX

Index